THE DREAM ENABLER

WORKBOOK

MATTHEW BURGESS

National Library of Australia Cataloguing-in-Publication entry

Creator: Burgess, Matthew, author.

Title: The Dream Enabler: Workbook/by Matthew Burgess;
   Illustrated by Dyan Burgess.

ISBN: 978-1-925406-07-8 (paperback)

ISBN: 978-1-925406-14-6 (Kindle)

ISBN: 978-1-925406-15-3 (ePub)

Subjects: Burgess, Matthew.
          Lawyers—Australia—Anecdotes.
          Practice of law—Australia—Anecdotes.
          Law—Australia—Anecdotes.

Other Creators/Contributors: Burgess, Dyan, illustrator.

Book Designer: Dimitrijevics, Otto

Dewey Number: 349.94

The Dream Enabler Workbook 2016

Copyright 2016 Matthew Burgess

The moral right of the author has been asserted. Without limiting the rights under copyright reserved above, no part of this publication may be reproduced, stored, or transmitted in any form or by any means, without prior written permission of both the copyright owner and the above publisher of this book.

While the author has made every effort to provide accurate Internet addresses at the time of publication, neither the publisher nor the author assumes any responsibility for errors, or for changes that occur after publication. Further the publisher does not have any control over and does not assume any responsibility for author or third-party websites or their content.

The information in this book is of a general nature, not intended to be specific professional advice. Please seek the opinion of a professional to advise you for your situation. The author's opinions are his own and do not represent the view of any other person, firm or entity. The author is not responsible for the accuracy or appropriateness of third-party comments or articles, including those of guest authors and editorial contributions. Any comments, letters, and other submissions are moderated and have been edited or withheld at the sole discretion of the author.

Published by D & M Fancy Pastry in 2016

Contents

Foreword xiii

ATTRIBUTE 1
PASSION 1
What do I truly 'get' (i.e. understand deeply)? 6
What do I truly 'love'? 7
What do I want above all else? 8
Where is the intersection? 9
If I fail 5 times, am I still truly passionate about continuing to search for success? 10
Is what I am truly passionate about polarising to the: 11

ATTRIBUTE 2
PERSISTENCE 13
What have I talent in that: 18
Is there a purpose to what I am willing to be stubborn about? 19
Can I be consistently consistent in: 20
Can I be consistently consistent in: 21
Is it time to quit … 22
Before I quit … 23

ATTRIBUTE 3
PURPOSE 25
Can I explain my purpose in a: 31
Is my purpose one which: 32
What does 'flow' *sound* like for me? 33
What does 'flow' *look* like for me? 34
When does 'flow' occur most readily for me? 35
Where does 'flow' occur most readily for me? 36
To create 'flow', do I: 37
Am I doing any of the following which will destroy 'flow': 39
I understand that to create 'flow', I must be: 41
If I survived a heart attack today, what would I change about how I treat my body? 46
If all of my knowledge were going to be redundant in 24 months, how would I approach learning? . . 47
If all others can hear what I say about them, how would I speak? 48
If my most important mentor were watching over me at all times, how would I act? 49
How do I improve on these key habits? 50
What am I doing to foster my: 52
'Redeeming things are not happiness and pleasure, but the deepest satisfactions that come out of a struggle'. 54
How can I access the genius of AND? 56

ATTRIBUTE 4
INCUBATE 59
Do I embrace the mantra, 'Is there another way?' 64
Have I asked the '5 Ys'? 65
"Good artists borrow. Great artists steal." — Pablo Picasso 67

The 5 most interesting things in other industries not currently in mine are: 68
How can I make competitors irrelevant due to: 69
How does the Internet leverage and enable my solution? 71
Am I deeply specialised, ideally in a niche, within a niche, within a niche? 72
What am I actively doing to disrupt the most successful part of my offering
    (knowing that if I am not disrupting it, someone else who cares nothing for me will be)? 73
What is the job I actually do for my customer and what problem do I solve for them? 74
The 10 most important things I do are: 76
The 10 least important things I do are: 78
Plot the 20 previous comments on the following curve:. 80
Where does the market see my solution sit in the value quadrant? 82
Where do my costs of production for my solution sit in the value quadrant? 84
Am I truly able to show my: 86
For every new idea, what's my MVP (Minimum Viable Product)? 87
My MVP: 88
How does my MVP: 90
Is my solution: 92
Does our firm honour the entrepreneur? 93
How am I a T?. 94
Is my disruptive solution: 96
My solution meets the 'McDonald's Model' as it:. 98
Simple is the key. Simple means less is more. 100
I foster associational thinking by: 102
I will write down everything that might be useful. Then read it. Then read it again.
    Then leave it. Then read it. Then repeat. 104
I know it is a fact that each of the following rewire my thinking and create magic: 106
My innovation to-do list:. 108

ATTRIBUTE 5
INSPIRE 111
The team around me: 116
My team knows I: 118
The rating of each person in my team on a scale of 1 to 10 for discretionary
    effort is as follows (10 being the highest) 120
How self-aware am I in: 121

ATTRIBUTE 6
INVEST 125
I demonstrate unwavering courage by: 130
My self-control is best when:. 131
Justice to me is: 132
I foster definiteness of decision by: 133
I create definiteness of plans by: 134
The top 10 ways I create more value than what I am paid for are: 135
I have re-scored myself on the emotional intelligence test in the last 90 days and … 137
Sympathy and understanding. 138
For me, mastery of detail means: 140
What steps can I take to more actively assume full responsibility? 141
Rituals 142
My NOT to-do list is as follows: 148
The focus checklist: 149
What I ingest either increases or decreases my: 151
My choices on ingestion have consequences EVERY time. 152

Real, whole foods increase my performance. Do I constantly track and choose alternatives
that are not:. 154
The daily checklist: 157

ATTRIBUTE 7
LAW. 161
10 times to be thinking slow 168
Decision tips table 169
Laws of attachment. I understand: 171
10 ways I can create 'hedonic disruption' (i.e. interrupting pleasant experiences)
in my life this week are: 173
Complete these sentences and then rewrite 30 times:. .175
I stopped falling into temptation by: 180
Everything is relative. 181
The power of 'free' is exponential. The top 5 ways I use free are:. 183
The 'Goldilocks principle' (i.e. giving the choice between 3 options) could be used
by me in the following areas:. 184

ATTRIBUTE 8
LEARNING. 187
Learning checklist: 192
Recomplete the following sentences: 193
Every task, every day, I will: 194
Solutions checklist: 196
Taleb's tips for the talented: 199
The 3 ways I intend to influence the future are: 200
With my solution, what elements of the model do I know with FULL CERTAINTY to be wrong? 201

ATTRIBUTE 9
LEVERAGE. 203
The long tail of the Internet 208
The business playing field is flat; how do I leverage:. 210
How can I create 'free' in my solution using: 212
Five ways I can versionise my solution are as follows
(i.e. similar solutions, sold to different market segments, with different prices): 214
Ten ways our team lives the mantra 'fail fast' are as follows: 216
Plot your solutions on the value monopoly matrix 218
What is my central message? 220
What is counterintuitive about my central message
(i.e. truly surprising and not already naturally occurring)? 221
Five steps to success: 222
What is the meaning of my solution?. 224
… plot your solution into 'Maslow's Pyramid' (the higher up the more meaning) 225
Am I … and my solution: 226
It is all about shipping. Shipping is all about having a one of one. 228
The one-page plan 230
Where else to learn?. 232

About the author 233
Acknowledgement. 235
Bibliography. 237

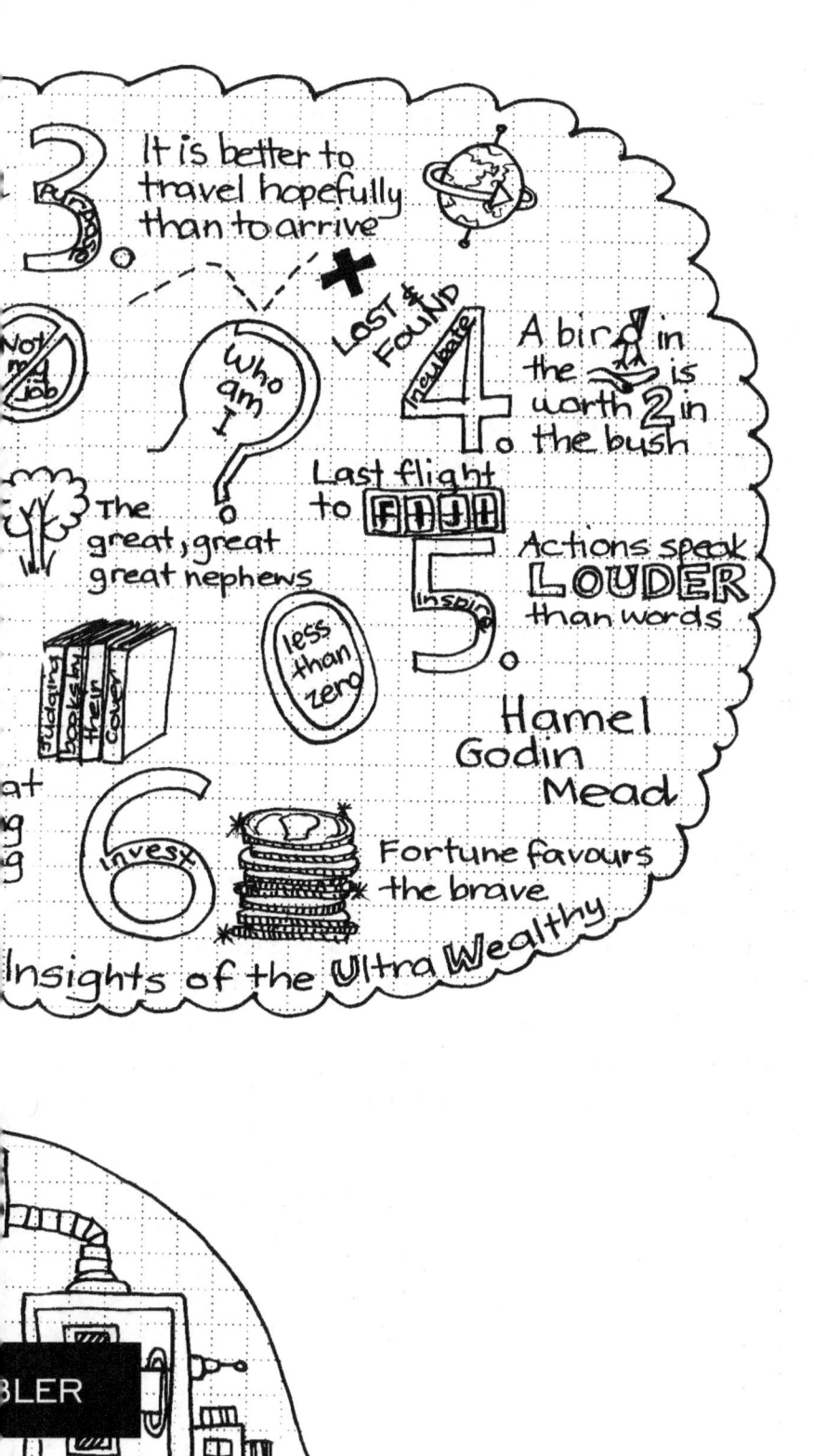

Matthew Burgess is certainly 'the lawyer to get when you don't want to deal with a lawyer'; yet he's far more than that—he is an incredibly deep thinker, and a great storyteller.

I couldn't put The Dream Enabler down, because not only do the stories of real people read like a novel, the lessons Matthew imparts in between are profound.

If you're a businessperson—in any field—you will find this book thought-provoking and valuable, and you'll see why one of Matthew's customers called him 'The Dream Enabler'–Indeed!

Ronald J. Baker
Founder, VeraSage Institute
Author of Implementing Value Pricing:
A Radical Model for Professional Firms,
and The Soul of Enterprise:
Dialogues on Business in the Knowledge Economy

I was lucky enough to cross paths with Matthew when looking for an inspirational speaker who could deliver an exciting keynote at the Bentleys Future Leaders conference. Matthew engaged our Future Leaders with energy and enthusiasm to dare to be different and make the change that is necessary for our future business. What fantastic true stories with real life situations. Wonderful tips and simple explanations. If you have always dreamt of it but never done it, read The Dream Enabler!

Heidi Mayhew-Sanders
Director, Human Resources
Bentleys Accountants

I have just completed 'The Dream Enabler' – the completion is a good sign in itself as I am very good at not finishing books if the large pile on my beside table is any indication. I am amazed that a practising lawyer would write a book on the keys to business success, particularly one that seeks to synthesise so much of the available learning from the authors in this area. There has obviously been an extraordinary amount of reading to have developed a range of remarkable insights into what drives businesses and individuals to succeed.

This book is a remarkable and unusual achievement.

Robert Clemente
Chief Executive
Television Education Network Pty Ltd

Drawing on thinking from some of the world's greatest philosophical and business minds, and his own impressive journey, Matthew's book reveals the key attributes for success for today's entrepreneur.

His captivating stories have you smiling, shaking your head in disbelief, and yearning for more.

Most importantly, his thought-provoking book will make you stop and reflect on your own life projection.

A must-read for all budding entrepreneurs or for those wanting to take the next leap in their entrepreneurial journey.

Katrina Walton
BAppSci HMS (Hons1), GCert OHS, MPH (Hons1), Cert IV TAA
Founder/Director/Workplace Wellness Strategist
Wellness Designs

I have had the pleasure of reading Matthew's book, "The Dream Enabler" and thoroughly enjoyed the stories of his experiences and sharing of his professional journey.

I have known Matthew Burgess for many years on both a personal and professional basis and found him to always be a true professional and one of the most respectful people I know.

Matthew has provided my family and business valuable advice and guidance on structuring and estate planning and remains our go to person for continuing advice and work in these areas.

Nic De Luca | *Managing Director*
De Luca Development & Construction
Chairman, Youngcare

The Dream Enabler is unlike any other book I've read.

Most books are 'linear' in form; you start here and it's a gentle journey to the end. This is anything but linear. And that's precisely what makes it so great.

One moment you're deeply engrossed in a beautifully told story about a High Net Worth person Matthew has worked with and learned from; the next moment you're 'transported' into a wonderful, brilliant almost barrister-like and superbly researched discussion on disrupting professions or on providing amazing service or on building world-class companies or on personal habits or … the list is huge.

Again, it's unlike ANY book I've read. And that's partly what makes it great. Hitherto untold deeply personal 'inside' stories topped with caring (and daring) insights.

And it's that 'caring' piece that really makes this great. This is not someone 'preaching' at you; it's someone involved in his own search sharing that uniqueness with you. And, just like this book, that's rare and worth grabbing hold of.

Paul Dunn
Chairman, B1G1 – Business for Good
5 times TEDx speaker, Global Lifetime Achievement Award for Service to the Accounting Profession

A selection of other feedback shared from those who have read 'The Dream Enabler' to date is as follows –

Extremely readable – in fact I read it from cover to cover in one sitting.

Enjoyed it very much – was engrossed from the start.

You are a natural storyteller; and what an exciting life you have led.

Extraordinary – may I please have three more copies now for gifts.

Fantastic read – I am starting to read it again to try and distil my own learning around some of the key concepts.

Exceptional effort consolidating the thinking of such a large range of books into one piece.

Foreword

SINCE THE EARLY 2000s, I have had the opportunity to work for many incredibly successful and inspirational people, including a significant percentage of the members of the various 'Rich Lists'. My roles have varied widely however, ultimately, have always involved helping people achieve a goal or vision that is part of their life's work.

Like most lawyers, I have had others attach labels to me over the years, including:

a   the baby-faced assassin
b   the lawyer to get when you don't want to deal with a lawyer
c   the 'www' (why the wealthy win) guy.

Undoubtedly there have been many other labels that, even if I knew of them, they would probably not be printable.

Someone, who never appeared on any list, coined the one that has meant the most to me.

She was a small business operator and we helped to ensure she had a structure that allowed her to survive and ultimately prosper during a difficult start-up phase. Her label for what I do is 'The dream enabler' and that is the theme and title of one of my books.

As set out in the foreword to 'The Dream Enabler', for as long as I can remember, the obsessive study of great thinkers has been my favourite pastime.

One aspect of this has been my evolving approach to 'common placing' – that is, the constant collection and ordering of the ideas of others.

Common placing has evolved, for me, from simply hoarding as many of my favourite books as possible, to cataloguing separately my favourite extracts, re-cataloguing extracts into disciplines and themes and to summarising the extracts into a centralised, personal 'bible' loosely titled 'brain food'.

Undoubtedly, everyone has their own learning style.

Successful entrepreneurs generally embrace one, or more, of the following concepts:

(1) You can only join the dots with hindsight.
(2) Actively creating serendipity is important.
(3) Fail fast.
(4) Deliver a 'MVP' – i.e. a minimum viable product, and then iterate, and iterate again.
(5) Embrace 'loose-tight' thinking.

This Workbook is designed to provide a framework for you to explore and achieve momentum in relation to each of the above concepts, leveraging the key attributes explained in detail in The Dream Enabler.

This Workbook is organised in the same order as the The Dream Enabler, that is, focusing on the following nine key attributes:

The three 'P's

(1) passion
(2) persistence
(3) purpose

The three 'I's

(4) incubate
(5) inspire
(6) invest

The three 'L's

(7) law
(8) learning
(9) leverage.

Unlike The Dream Enabler, the content in this Workbook is deliberately brief. The Workbook is focused on questions, rather than answers

The Workbook is designed to provide a catalyst, or starting point, for your personal journey in each of the 9 attributes explored in The Dream Enabler.

While it is a companion to the book, there is certainly no reason that you need have read The Dream Enabler before exploring the Workbook.

This said, in areas where you are wanting to deepen your understanding about particular concepts, the comparative chapter in The Dream Enabler will provide the foundation for further learning. Alternatively, down load your free copy of the Reference Guide from:

www.thedreamenabler.com.au/referenceguide

There is space throughout the Workbook for you to explore and crystallise your own thoughts, capture themes and cross-reference other ideas.

The Workbook is written to you, as the individual reader, even though the vast majority of the concepts explored can apply equally to a business, firm or organisation.

The Workbook's design is agnostic in relation to how you use it.

A lineal, methodical approach can be adopted.

Alternatively, adopt a completely random path, following threads as you get to them. Otherwise, simply ignore entire sections if they do not, at the relevant juncture, capture your attention.

Ultimately, my hope for this Workbook is that it facilitates your personal focused, common placing, and that in turn provides the foundation for your continued learning and realising of your dreams.

ATTRIBUTE 1

PASSION

> "Reasonable men adapt themselves to the world. Unreasonable men adapt the world to themselves. That is why all progress depends on unreasonable men."
>
> — *George Bernard Shaw*

Passion – why

The wealthy understand that relationships and feelings are what are fundamentally important – particularly in comparison with things and considered thought.

What do I truly 'get' (i.e. understand deeply)?

What do I truly 'love'?

What do I want above all else?

Where is the intersection?

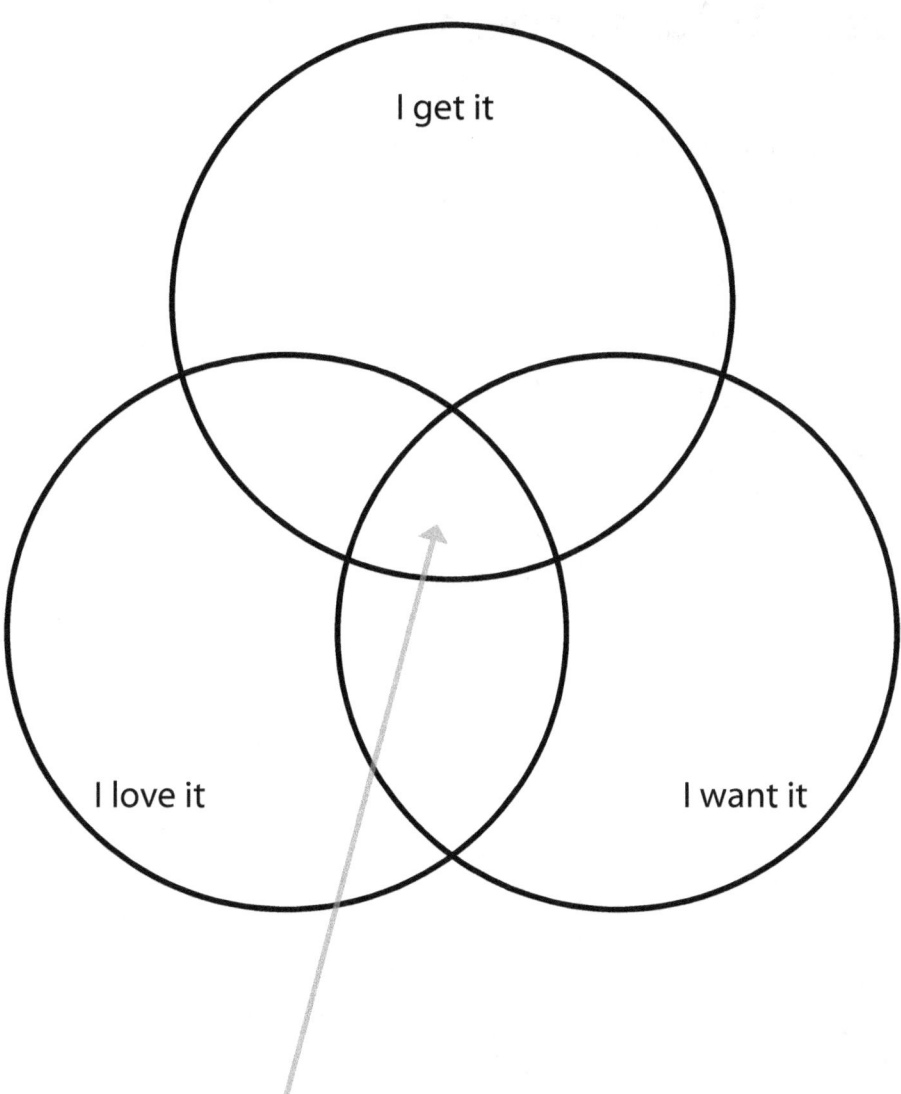

Where I need to be

If I fail 5 times, am I still truly passionate about continuing to search for success?

What about failing:

☐ 10 times

☐ 50 times

☐ 100 times

☐ 500 times

Is what I am truly passionate about polarising to the:

☐ Machine/Establishment

☐ Competitors

☐ Friends

☐ Family

☐ Enemies

☐ All of the above

ATTRIBUTE 2

PERSISTENCE

> "Great spirits have always encountered violent opposition from mediocre minds."
>
> — *Albert Einstein*

Persistence – why

The only thing that ultimately distinguishes between success and failure is persistent persistence.

What have I talent in that:

☐ Requires deep skills

☐ Is valuable to others

☐ I am willing to invest 1,000 hours every year for 10 years

Is there a purpose to what I am willing to be stubborn about?

Can I be consistently consistent in:

Actions

Values

Can I be consistently consistent in:

Purpose

Standards of performance and delivery

Is it time to quit ...

☐ Am I panicking because of pressure?

☐ What do those in my tribe really think of what I am doing?

☐ Objectively, what progress am I making?

Before I quit ...

☐ What is the objective evidence of my belief?

☐ Is there a less negative theory for my belief?

☐ What objectively are the consequences of quitting?

☐ Can I delay further thought for 15 days before making a final decision?

ATTRIBUTE 3

PURPOSE

> **He who has a why can endure any how.**
>
> — *Friedrich Nietzsche*

Purpose – why

As the saying goes, those who chase two rabbits, catch neither.
An ability to aspire to a meaning far greater than oneself is the most powerful of characteristics.

Can I explain my purpose in a:

Paragraph

Sentence

Word

Is my purpose one which:

☐ Is focused on the long term

☐ Embraces self-control

☐ Is bigger than anyone or anything

What does 'flow' *sound* like for me?

What does 'flow' *look* like for me?

When does 'flow' occur most readily for me?

Where does 'flow' occur most readily for me?

To create 'flow', do I:

☐ Set an overall goal with sub goals

☐ Measure my progress

☐ Concentrate without ANY interruptions

☐ Focus my skills on the goal

☐ Develop strategies to persist through 'the boring bits'

Am I doing any of the following which will destroy 'flow':

☐ Watching TV

☐ Consuming internet/social media/newspapers

☐ Substance usage

☐ Speaking before thinking

I understand that to create 'flow', I must be:

☐ Challenged

☐ Concentrating

☐ Goal orientated

☐ Looking for feedback

- ☐ Deeply and effortlessly involved

- ☐ In control

- ☐ Self-disciplined

- ☐ Ignoring time

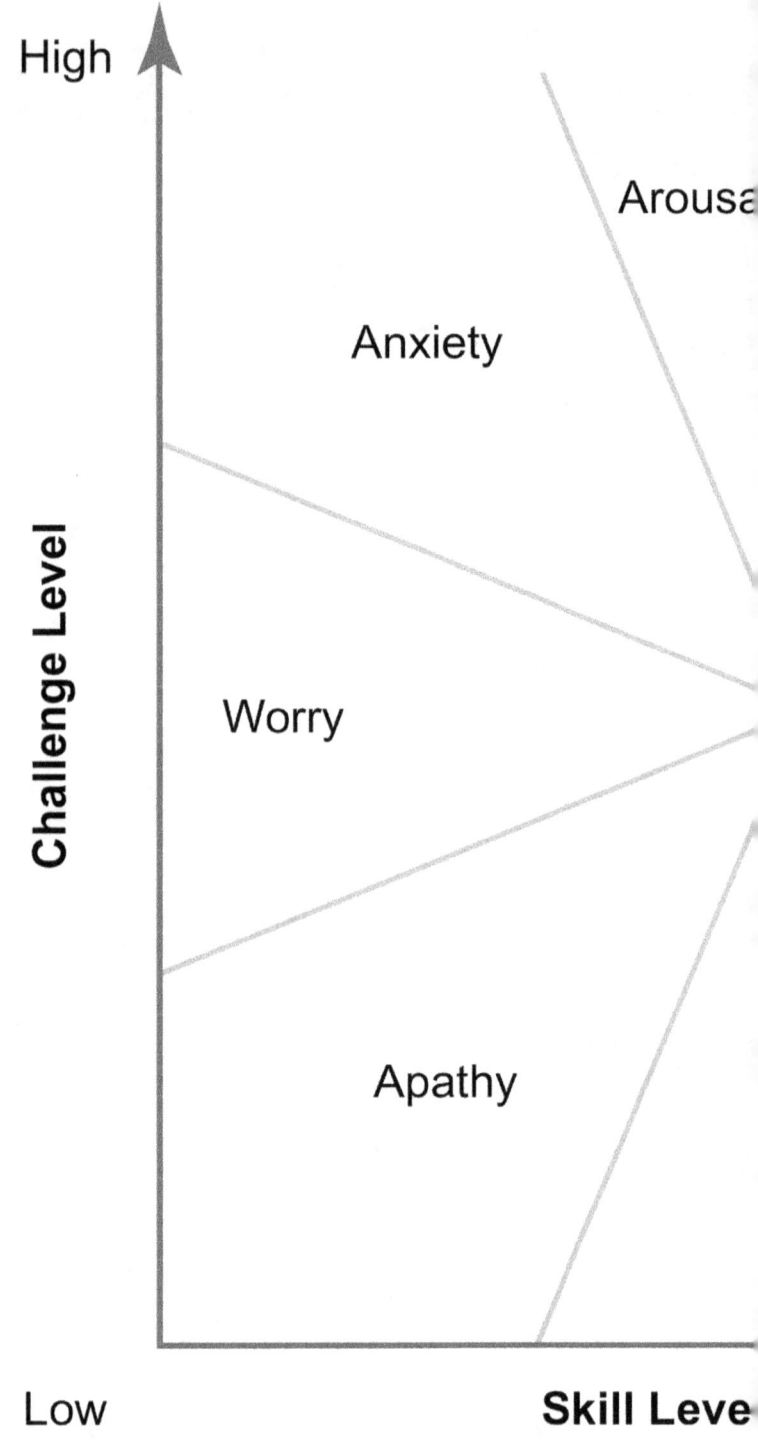

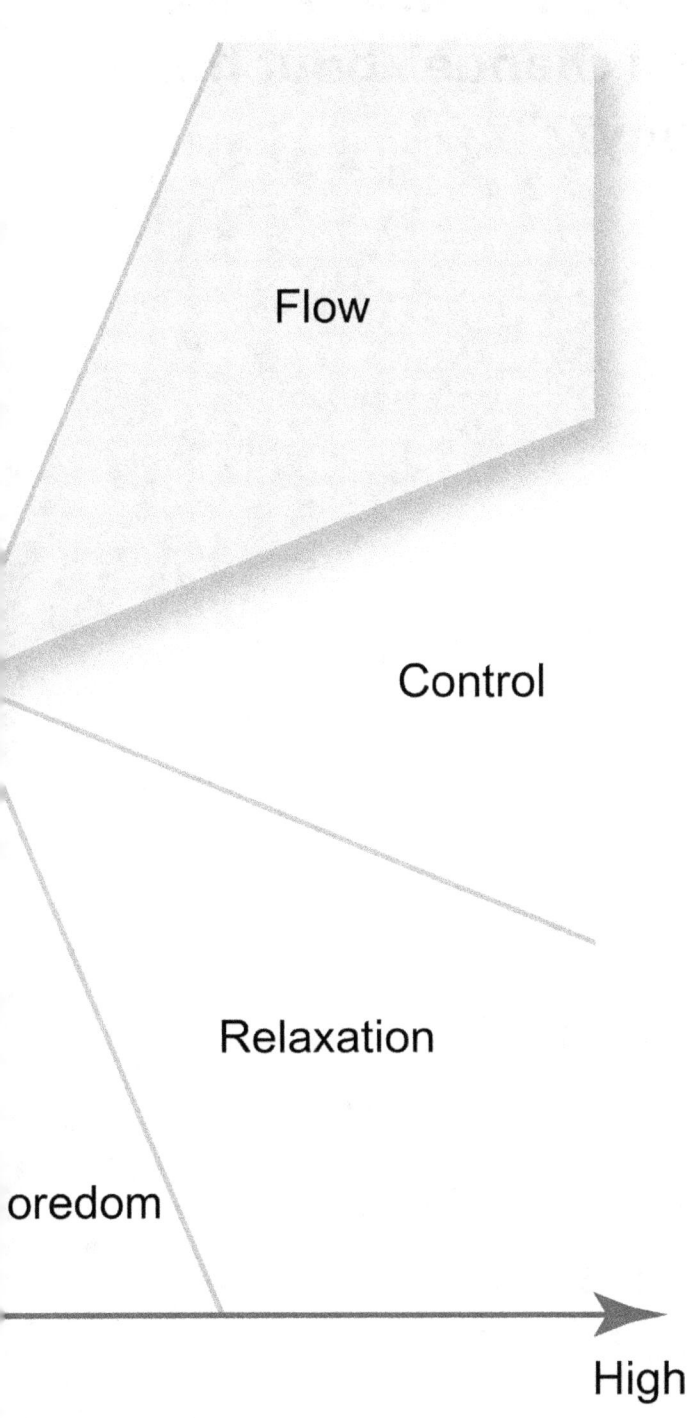

If I survived a heart attack today, what would I change about how I treat my body?

If all of my knowledge were going to be redundant in 24 months, how would I approach learning?

If all others can hear what I say about them, how would I speak?

If my most important mentor were watching over me at all times, how would I act?

How do I improve on these key habits?

Habit	Steps to take
Be Proactive	
Begin with the End in Mind	
Put First Things First	
Think Win Win	
Seek First to Understand, Then to be Understood	
Synergise	
Sharpen the Saw	

What am I doing to foster my:

☐ Wisdom

☐ Courage

☐ Love

☐ Justice

☐ Temperance

☐ Spirit

'Redeeming things are not happiness and pleasure, but the deepest satisfactions that come out of a struggle'.

Discuss.

continued …

How can I access the genius of AND?

1	+
core ideology	AND
continuity	AND
conservative	AND
stability	AND
predictability	AND
heritage	AND
fundamentals	AND

1	=	3
simultaneous progress		
change		
progression		
revolution		
chaos		
renewal		
craziness		

ATTRIBUTE 4

INCUBATE

> **I skate to where the puck is going to be, not where it has been.**
> — *Wayne Gretzky*

Incubate – why

For many, incubation is simply referred
to as innovation.
The truly wealthy understand that innovation
of itself is insufficient. There must be the constant
and disciplined trialling of new concepts
in a manner that is designed to achieve successful
new business models.
In many respects, innovation is a necessary, but not
a sufficient, building block of incubation.
Ultimately, innovators are thinkers;
incubators are doers.

Do I embrace the mantra, 'Is there another way?'

Have I asked the '5 Ys'?

☐ Why do people choose me?

☐ Why don't people choose me?

☐ Why will people continue to choose me?

☐ Why might people choose others?

☐ Why would people recommend me to others?

'Good artists borrow. Great artists steal.' — Pablo Picasso

Discuss.

The 5 most interesting things in other industries not currently in mine are:

1.

2.

3.

4.

5.

How can I make competitors irrelevant due to:

☐ Usability

☐ Price points

☐ Cost of production

☐ Two of the above

☐ All of the above (= success)

How does the Internet leverage and enable my solution?

Am I deeply specialised, ideally in a niche, within a niche, within a niche?

What am I actively doing to disrupt the most successful part of my offering (knowing that if I am not disrupting it, someone else who cares nothing for me will be)?

What is the job I actually do for my customer and what problem do I solve for them?

The 10 most important things I do are:

1.

2.

3.

4.

5.

6.

7.

8.

9.

10.

The 10 least important things I do are:

1.

2.

3.

4.

5.

6.

7.

8.

9.

10.

Plot the 20 previous comments on

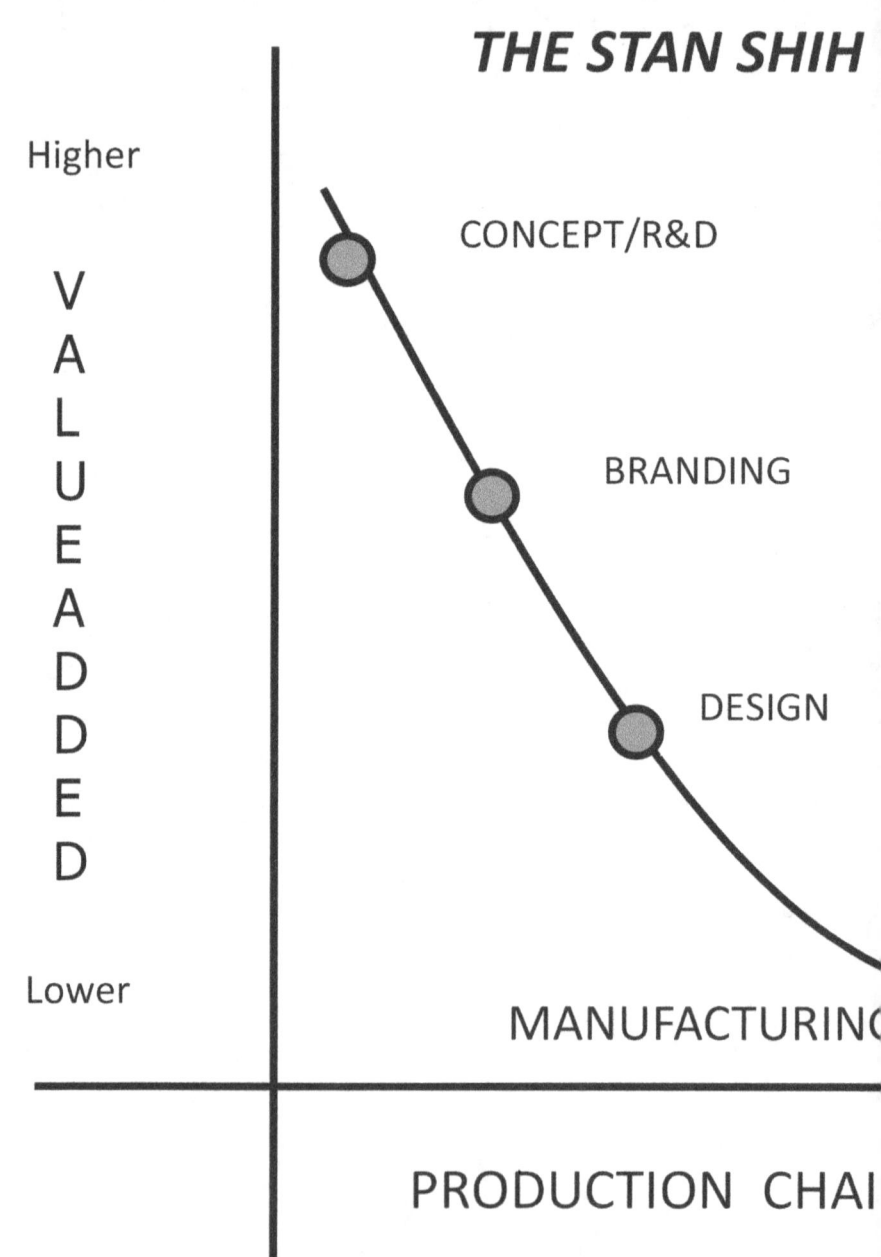

the following curve:

SMILE CURVE

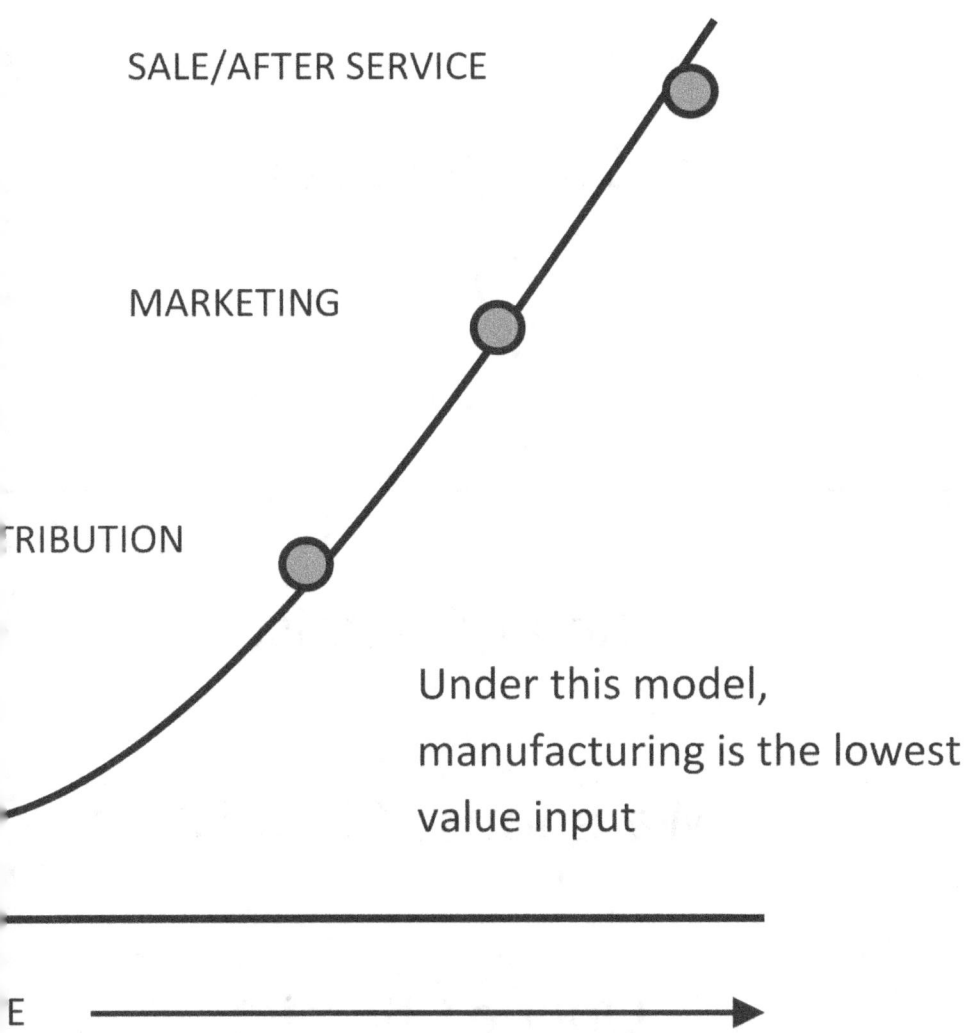

SALE/AFTER SERVICE

MARKETING

DISTRIBUTION

Under this model, manufacturing is the lowest value input

Where does the market see my

Brain Surgeon

Retail Chemist
↓
Warehouse Chemist
↓
Online Chemist

solution sit in the value quadrant?

Physiotherapist

Nurse

Where do my costs of production for

Brain Surgeon

Retail Chemist
⭣
Warehouse Chemist
⭣
Online Chemist

my solution sit in the value quadrant?

Physiotherapist

Nurse

Am I truly able to show my:

☐ Differentiation

☐ Value proposition

☐ Delivery that is difficult to replicate

For every new idea, what's my MVP (Minimum Viable Product)?

My MVP:

☐ Monetises quickly

☐ Is quick to launch

☐ Is launched so early that I am embarrassed; at least until v2 is out

☐ Leverages existing skills

☐ Has support to push through 'apparent fails'

How does my MVP:

☐ Challenge the assumed non-negotiables of heritage business models

☐ Embrace trends in unrelated industries yet to take off in my space

☐ Leverage what I know, not what I do

☐ Do an important job for my customer even if they did not previously know the job was needed

Is my solution:

☐ Simple

☐ Reliable

☐ Convenient

☐ Deliverable at low margins

Does our firm honour the entrepreneur?

☐ Keeping them at the centre of the business

☐ Keeping management in check

☐ Repelling bureaucracy

How am I a T?

Broad knowledge across a

range of ideally unrelated fields ⟶

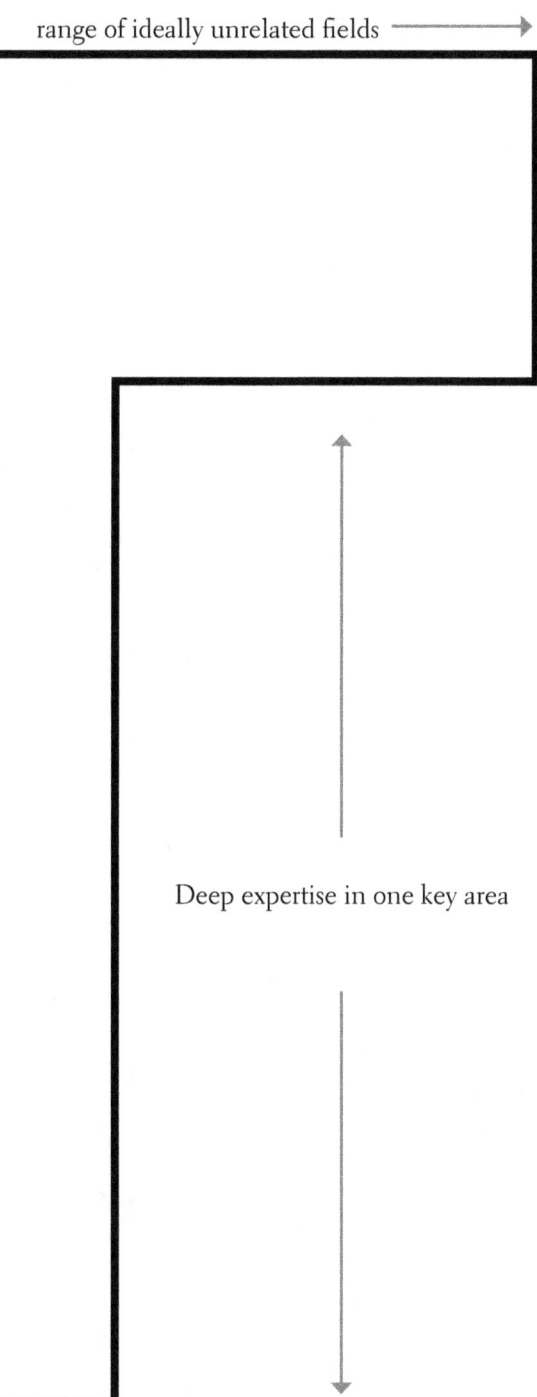

Deep expertise in one key area

Is my disruptive solution:

☐ Free of all management

☐ Led by specialists

☐ Completely autonomous with resource allocation

☐ Judged on net profit over at least 3 years

☐ Supported, without exception, by leaders of heritage business

☐ Solely focused on the MVP mantra

My solution meets the 'McDonald's Model' as it:

☐ Simplifies

☐ Has consistent quality

☐ Requires only well-trained (not experienced) team members

☐ Decreases price, increases value, or both

☐ Improves convenience

☐ Radically increases the volume of customers who can be served

Simple is the key. Simple means less is more.

Discuss.

continued…

I foster associational thinking by:

☐ Questioning incessantly

☐ Learning from others

☐ Experimenting

☐ Meeting people

☐ All of the above (= success)

I will write down everything that might be useful. Then read it. Then read it again. Then leave it. Then read it. Then repeat.

(Write the above down 20 times)

1.

2.

3.

4.

5.

6.

7.

8.

9.

10.

11.

12.

13.

14.

15.

16.

17.

18.

19.

20.

I know it is a fact that each of the following rewire my thinking and create magic:

☐ Sleeping

☐ Walking

☐ Eating real food

☐ Drinking real water

☐ Exercising

☐ Condensed deep reading blocks

☐ Networking with a diverse range of people

My innovation to-do list:

- Write down EVERY THING
- Cultivate hunches
- Go for walks
- Make mistakes
- Keep messy journals
- Love serendipity

- Have multiple hobbies
- Follow the links
- Foster a liquid network
- Enable others to build on my ideas
- Tangle a bank of learnings
- Borrow Recycle Reinvent Steal

ATTRIBUTE 5

INSPIRE

❝A man convinced against his will
is of the same opinion still. ❞
— *William Blake*

Inspire – why

Truly wealthy people have an innate ability to inspire others. Importantly, those who are inspired will almost always go on to inspire others.

The team around me:

☐ Is all more talented than me in their core strengths

☐ Demands excellence and offloads passengers

☐ Have the opportunity to stretch for a 'BHAG' – i.e. a big, hairy, audacious goal

☐ Engage in fearless debate and a disciplined search for the future

My team knows I:

☐ Expect great things from them

☐ Will create positive emotions if they are genuinely deserved in a ratio of at least 3:1

☐ Ignore cosmetic feel good outcomes

☐ Rarely take myself too seriously

☐ Strive to be self-aware

The rating of each person in my team on a scale of 1 to 10 for discretionary effort is as follows (10 being the highest)

	Team Member	*Discretionary Effort Score*
A		
B		
C		
D		
E		
F		
G		

How self-aware am I in:

☐ Understanding my strengths and weaknesses

☐ Constantly innovating

☐ Engaging those around me using a positive attitude

☐ Creating energy and empowerment with a BHAG

My Emotional Intelligence self-awareness test

Item	Definition	Hallmarks	Score out of 10
Self-Awareness	✓ The ability to recognise and understand your moods, emotions, and drives, as well as their effect on others	✓ Self confidence ✓ Realistic self-assessment ✓ Self-deprecating sense of humour	
Self-Regulation	✓ The ability to control or redirect disruptive impulses and moods ✓ The propensity to suspend judgement – to think before acting	✓ Trust worthiness and integrity ✓ Comfort with ambiguity ✓ Openness to change	
Motivation	✓ A passion to work for reasons that go beyond money or status ✓ A propensity to pursue goals with energy and persistence	✓ Strong drive to achieve ✓ Optimism, even in the face of failure ✓ Organisational commitment	
Empathy	✓ The ability to understand the emotional makeup of other people ✓ Skill in treating people according to their emotional reactions	✓ Expertise in building and retaining talent ✓ Cross cultural sensitivity ✓ Service to customers and customers	
Social Skill	✓ Proficiency in managing relationships and building networks ✓ An ability to find common ground and build rapport	✓ Effectiveness in leading change Persuasiveness ✓ Expertise in building and leading terms	

ATTRIBUTE 6

INVEST

> **We want to create the business model that blows up our current business model, because if we don't, somebody else will.**
> — *Paul LeBlanc*

Invest – why

Change is the only certainty. Investing for the future today is the only pathway to success tomorrow.
The more that can be invested early and the more unwavering the discipline of that investment the more the magic of compounding can take place.

I demonstrate unwavering courage by:

My self-control is best when:

Justice to me is:

I foster definiteness of decision by:

I create definiteness of plans by:

The top 10 ways I create more value than what I am paid for are:

1.

2.

3.

4.

5.

6.

7.

8.

9.

10.

I have re-scored myself on the emotional intelligence test in the last 90 days and …

Date	Cumulative Score

Sympathy and understanding.

Discuss.

continued …

For me, mastery of detail means:

What steps can I take to more actively assume full responsibility?

Rituals

	Ritual	Examples Generally
1	Solitude	a. Spare room or peaceful corner b. Same time every day c. Walking every day
2	Physicality	a. Prepare your body and prepare your mind b. Vigorous exercise every day c. Vigorous walking d. Yoga e. Breathe with purpose two to three times a day
3	Live nourishment	Alive rather than dead foods – eat food created through the interaction of sun, air, soil and water: vegetables, fruits and unprocessed nuts and grains.
4	Abundant knowledge	a. Be a student for life b. Read nourishing material for 30 minutes a day to improve yourself and your quality of life c. Study the great books.
5	Personal reflection	a. Contemplation b. Habit of thinking c. Review all actions at the end of each day with a view to correcting negative responses – the only way to improve tomorrow is to know what went wrong today d. Happiness comes from good judgment, good judgement comes from experience and experience comes from bad judgment.

Specifically Me

	Ritual	Examples Generally
6	Early awakening	a Six hours sleep is sufficient b Sleep is nothing more than a habit c Embrace the sun (include sunbathing) d The 10-minute period before and after sleep most profoundly influences the subconscious mind e In every situation, consider how you would respond if the day were your last.
7	Music	Music is powerful.
8	Spoken word	a Use written and verbal affirmations (e.g. repeating a mantra) b Self-image is critical – never act inconsistently.
9	Congruent character	a Take daily incremental action to build character b Actions come together to form habits; habits lead to destiny c Sow a thought to reap an action, sow an action to reap a habit, sow a habit to reap a character, sow a character to reap your destiny d Congruent principles are industry, compassion, humility, patience, honesty and courage. When all actions are congruent and aligned with these principles, there will be inner harmony and peace.

Specifically Me

	Ritual	Examples Generally
10	Simplicity	a. Live a simple life b. Never live in the thick of thin things – focus on priorities c. Life will be uncluttered, rewarding and peaceful d. The key is not to make happiness contingent on finding anything in particular (e.g. a pot of gold) e. Nothing in extreme, everything in moderation.

Specifically Me

My NOT to-do list is as follows:

The focus checklist:

☐ Key perspective – MVP solutions

☐ Concentrate on concentrating

☐ Prioritise daily

☐ Choose not to time waste

☐ Choose not to procrastinate

☐ Create momentum

☐ Choose not to be interrupted

What I ingest either increases or decreases my:

☐ Perception of what I can achieve

☐ Ability to achieve

My choices on ingestion have consequences EVERY time.

Discuss.

continued …

Real, whole foods increase my performance. Do I constantly track and choose alternatives that are not:

☐ Processed

☐ Packaged

☐ Filled with carbohydrates

☐ Laden with sugars

☐ Pumped full of chemicals

☐ Stored for months

Blues – blueberries, blackberries, cabbage, cranberries and grapes

Reds – apples, tomatoes, strawberries, raspberries, red peppers, goji, radishes, chilly peppers, salmon

Greens – broccoli, asparagus, artichokes, spinach, sprouts, lettuce, kale, bok choy, avocado, beans

The daily checklist:

☐ Be near moving water, or at least stream it via my stereo

☐ Move more

☐ Look out the window

☐ Get outside

☐ Use exercise to become physically tired

☐ Alternate between handheld dictation, mainframe computer work, handheld interaction and physical paper

ATTRIBUTE 7

LAW

> **All truth passes through three stages. First, it is ridiculed. Second, it is violently opposed. Third, it is accepted as being self-evident.**
> — *Arthur Schopenhauer*

Law – why

A deep understanding of universal laws has always been fundamental to success.
As society becomes more complex, the need to understand and apply these laws has and will continue to be critical.

No	Thinking Fast	Thinking Slow
1.	Intuitive	Deliberate
2.	Automatic	Effortful
3.	'Easy'	'Hard'
4.	A little energy	Very draining
5.	Risky when deep thinking needed	Undermined by assumptions

Discuss.

continued …

10 times to be thinking slow

(1) Halo effect: judgements about character can be influenced by an overall impression of the person

(2) Framing effect: people react differently to a particular choice depending on whether it is presented as a loss or as a gain

(3) Confirmation bias: (also called confirmatory bias or my side bias) the tendency of people to favour information that confirms their beliefs or hypotheses

(4) Outcome bias: error made in evaluating the quality of a decision when the outcome of that decision is already known

(5) Hindsight bias: also known as the 'knew-it-all-along' effect or creeping determinism – the inclination to see events that have already occurred as being more predictable than they were before they took place

(6) Anchoring effect: relying too heavily on the first piece of information received

(7) Focusing illusion: placing too much importance on one aspect of an event, causing an error in accurately predicting the utility of a future outcome

(8) The Florida effect: the use of 'priming' to put someone in a psychological state that affects their actions without their conscious knowledge

(9) Under the influence: of drugs (legal or illicit) or any form of mental illness

(10) Belief perseverance: the tendency not to reverse any opinion once it is fully formed

Decision tips table

Decision Type	Approach
Straightforward	(1) Deliberate analysis (2) Methodical (3) Clinical
Complex	(1) Reduced to simplest elements (2) Rationally analyse patterns (3) Default to intuition, actively filtering out assumption risks

Discuss.

continued …

Laws of attachment.
I understand:

☐ The effort I apply does not change reality, it only changes my perception of reality

☐ More my labour = more my love

☐ My love for something does not mean those around me feel the same

☐ If I fail to complete something I strive for, I will become overly unattached

10 ways I can create 'hedonic disruption' (i.e. interrupting pleasant experiences) in my life this week are:

1.

2.

3.

4.

5.

6.

7.

8.

9.

10.

Complete these sentences and then rewrite 30 times:

100% is E _ _ Y   99% is H _ _ D

1.

2.

3.

4.

5.

6.

7.

8.

9.

10.

11.

12.

13.

14.

15.

16.

17.

18.

19.

20.

21.

22.

23.

24.

25.

26.

27.

28.

29.

30.

I stopped falling into temptation by:

☐ Doing the 'hardest' thing first each day

☐ Physically removing temptations, particularly from 12.00pm each day

☐ Delaying taking the temptation for as long as possible

Everything is relative.

Discuss.

continued …

The power of 'free' is exponential. The top 5 ways I use free are:

1.

2.

3.

4.

5.

The 'Goldilocks principle' (i.e. giving the choice between 3 options) could be used by me in the following areas:

ATTRIBUTE 8

LEARNING

> **The great disadvantage of experience is the loss of the stupidity and absurd bravery that comes with not knowing what works ... when you don't know what works you will try anything.**
> — *Joe Calloway*

Learning – why

Dedication to lifelong learning is a fundamental key to success.

Learning checklist:

☐ My success depends on being a student for life

☐ I search for new ways to do OLD things

☐ I search for new ways to do NEW things

☐ I live by the '5 Ys'

☐ A mantra I embrace is – 'Is there another way?'

Recomplete the following sentences:

100% is E _ _ Y

99% is H _ _ D

Every task, every day, I will:

☐ Do only one thing at a time

☐ Complete as fully as possible

☐ Eliminate ALL external stimuli and interruptions (other than music)

☐ Concentrate on concentrating

☐ Have 'worry breaks' and write down anything concerning me

Solutions checklist:

My solutions are all of the following:

☐ Functional

☐ Designed attractively

☐ Underpinned by an engaging story

☐ Create a symphony

☐ Logical

☐ Empathetic

☐ Serious

☐ Playful

☐ Create meaning

Taleb's tips for the talented:

☐ No TV, radio or news

☐ Allocate new found spare time to reading and learning

☐ Take sabbaticals to create my 'T' skill set

The 3 ways I intend to influence the future are:

1.

2.

3.

With my solution, what elements of the model do I know with FULL CERTAINTY to be wrong?

ATTRIBUTE 9

LEVERAGE

> "When I was a boy of 14, my father was so ignorant I could hardly stand to have the old man around. But when I got to be 21, I was astonished at how much the old man had learned in seven years."
> — *Mark Twain*

Leverage – why

The most influential factor in any form of success is the ability to create leverage. While this has always been the case, technological advances have exponentially reinforced the principle and are likely to continue to do so.

The long tail of the Internet

Niche more important that hits

Look for niches within niches

Markets are driven by the niches despite attention the hits get

> Costs of delivering to a niche tracking to zero

> Niches combined create markets the size of hits

The business playing field is flat; how do I leverage:

☐ Abundant information

☐ Ever increasing quality

☐ Accelerated life cycles

☐ Trend to commoditisation

How can I create 'free' in my solution using:

☐ Cross subsidies

☐ Third party fees (e.g. advertising)

☐ Freemium (i.e. free with paid upgrades)

☐ Non-money market (e.g. discussion groups)

Five ways I can versionise my solution are as follows (i.e. similar solutions, sold to different market segments, with different prices):

1.

2.

3.

4.

5.

Ten ways our team lives the mantra 'fail fast' are as follows:

1.

2.

3.

4.

5.

6.

7.

8.

9.

10.

Plot your solutions on the value monopoly matrix

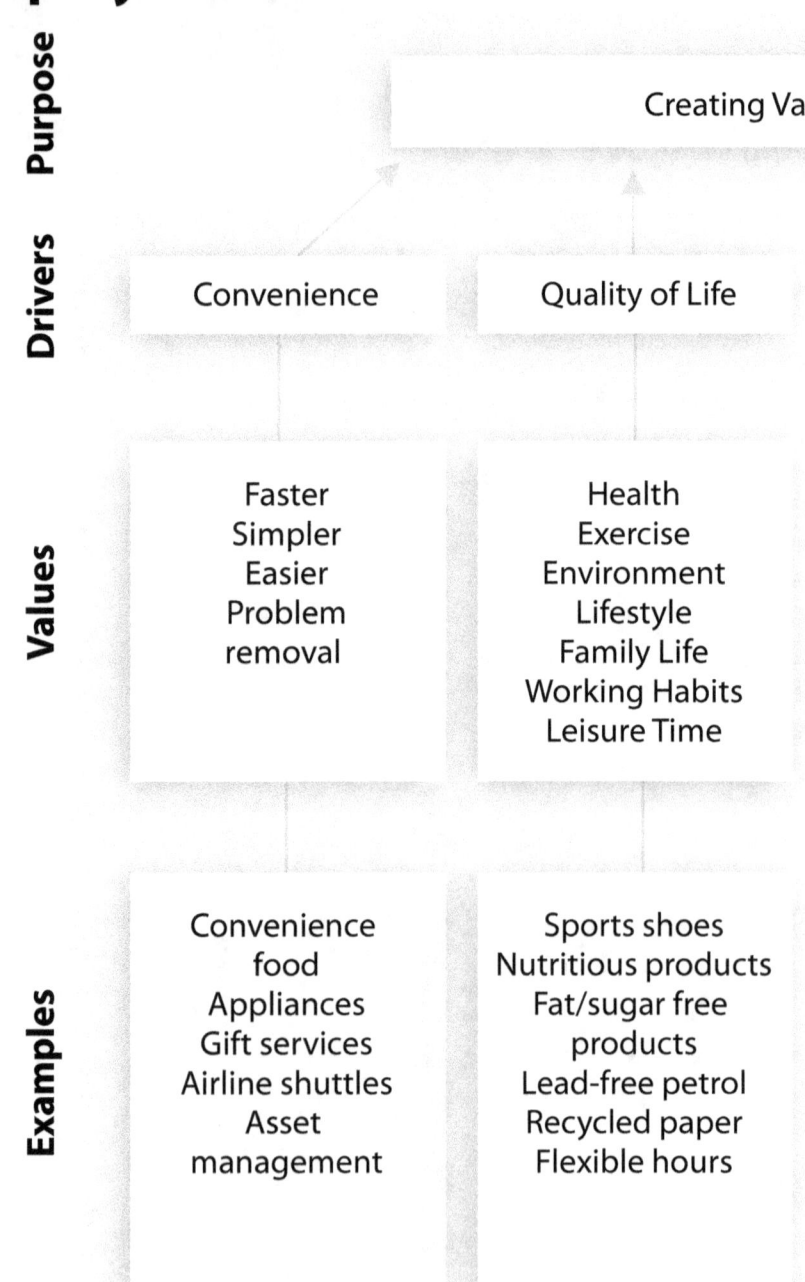

```
                    Monopoly
                   ↗         ↖
         Self Importance      Distraction

         Self Esteem           Peace
         Others Esteem         Stimulation
         Recognition           Comfort
         Exclusivity           Enjoyment


         Fashion items         Religion
         Places                Television
         Prestige symbols      Alcohol/
         Awards/titles/         cigarettes
          insignia             Entertainment
         Restricted            Leisure/tourism
          groupings            Karaoke
         Special occasions     Getaways
         Name-dropping
```

What is my central message?

What is counterintuitive about my central message (i.e. truly surprising and not already naturally occurring)?

Five steps to success:

(1) Make people pay attention – be unexpected
(2) Create something to remember – have a message
(3) Cause others to believe – be credible
(4) Cause others to care – create meaning
(5) Live your solution – have a story

Discuss.

continued …

What is the meaning of my solution?

Self-
Actualisation
(problem solving)

Esteem (confidence, achievement)

Social (love, well-being)

Security (resources, family)

Physiological (air, food, water)

… plot your solution into 'Maslow's Pyramid' (the higher up the more meaning)

Am I ... and my solution:

	What
1.	Likable
2.	Connected with people
3.	Solving a problem
4.	Building a trust
5.	Cause positive emotional experiences

Why & How

It is all about shipping. Shipping is all about having a one of one.

Discuss.

continued …

The one-page plan

Accountability
1. daily
2. the who
3. 1 of 1 (rinse + repeat)

Schedule (weekly – the when):

Action (90 days – the how):

Goals (yearly – the what):

Targets (3–5 years – the where):

Purpose (last life of leader – the why):

Core Values (last forever – the should):

Where else to learn?

(1) Re-read (or read) The Dream Enabler (www.thedreamenabler.com.au)
(2) Download your free copy of the Dream Enabler reference guide – www.thedreamenabler.com.au/referenceguide
(3) Apply to become DEFT member – www.thedreamenabler.com.au/deftmember – the Dream Enabler Forum Team

About the author

Having the opportunity to help clients realise their dreams is what Matthew is most passionate about.

As Matthew always works in conjunction with trusted advisers (whether it be accountants, financial advisers or other lawyers) and their clients, finding ways to fundamentally improve the value received by those advisers, and in turn their clients, has led him to develop numerous game changing models.

Examples include providing guaranteed upfront fixed pricing, founding what is widely regarded as Australia's first virtual law firm, and more recently, developing a platform that gives advisers access to market leading advice and support for less than $1 a week.

Matthew's specialisation in tax, structuring, asset protection, estate and succession planning has seen him recognised by most leading industry associations including the Tax Institute, the Weekly Tax Bulletin and since 2014 in the Australian 'Best Lawyers' list for trusts and estates and since 2015 in 'Doyles' for taxation.

In 2015 Matthew won the individual award on the prestigious LexisNexis – Legal Innovation Index.

Work is one aspect of his life Matthew loves, so there is no need to be constantly searching for 'balance'. His other great loves are:

1. Family – they are profiled in various ways through the series of children's books he has written under the pseudonym 'Lily Burgess' – see www.wordsfromdaddysmouth.com.au and various TV commercials.
2. Health – aside from being a foodie and swimming at least a 5km a week, Matthew installed a stand up workstation in 2007 and among a few other lifestyle choices, it changed his life.
3. Learning – going cold turkey on television and most forms of media in late 2005 has radically increased Matthew's ability to study the great authors and inspired him to publish a book that explores the concept of 'true success' – see www.thedreamenabler.com.au

Acknowledgement

The Dream Enabler book, and in turn this Workbook, are the result of contributions from countless people, each who I thank in a general sense.

More particularly:

1. All of the customers I have been fortunate enough to assist over the years have had significant influence on me personally, and obviously, the stories of a number of them form the foundation of this book.
2. While I only know a handful of the authors listed in the bibliography of The Dream Enabler, personally, all of them also have had a significant influence on me, and again obviously, this book.
3. There have been countless people involved, as with any book production, in reviewing, editing, designing and ultimately publishing it. The contribution of each and every person is very gratefully acknowledged.
4. The team of people that I work with at View have inspired me virtually every day for many years now. Personal thanks to each of them.
5. Finally, very deep and personal thanks to my family, and in particular, my immediate family. This Workbook is a result of countless weeks I have spent away from them reading, researching, collating and writing. It also signifies the end, at least for the time being, of a project that in its current form has been around 6 months of focused effort and energy.

Bibliography

This book is based on one of my previous publications—'The Dream Enabler'.

The Dream Enabler sets out a detailed bibliography listing all of the authors and books who provided the foundation for both that book, and in turn, ultimately this book.

A free copy of the bibliography is available via another of my books—'The Dream Enabler Reference Guide'—see:

http://www.thedreamenabler.com.au/referenceguide/

In this book ('The Dream Enabler Workbook'), there are a number of instances where the material set out is directly sourced from the works of others, as detailed in the abovementioned bibliography.

In summary, the ultimate sources (in the order they appear) in this book are as follows:

1. The 'flow' diagram—Andre Ivanchuk, interpreting the work of Mihaly Csikszentmihalyi;
2. The 'Seven Habits of Highly Effective People' by Stephen Covey;
3. The Genius of 'and'—Jim Collins and Jerry Porras;
4. '5 Whys'—Sakichi Toyoda (as popularised by Toyota Motor Corporation);
5. Professional service delivery business models quadrant—David Maister;
6. 'BHAG'—Jim Collins and Jerry Porras;
7. Emotional Intelligence—Daniel Goleman;
8. Rituals—Robin Sharma;
9. Real food—Tom Rath;
10. Thinking, fast and slow—Daniel Kahneman;

11. Thinking slow—Charlie Munger;
12. 'The Long Tail' and 'Free'—Chris Anderson;
13. 'Monopoly matrix'—Edward de bono and John Lyons;
14. The Maslow pyramid—Abraham Maslow, although there is no evidence to suggest Maslow actually designed this pyramid, it is generally attributed to him because of his work in the area;
15. 'Shipping'—Seth Godin; and
16. The one-page business plan pyramid—Verne Harnish.

www.ingramcontent.com/pod-product-compliance
Lightning Source LLC
Chambersburg PA
CBHW070326240426
43671CB00013BA/2376